Grades 1–2 Math

MONOPOLY™ Activity Book—Grades 1–2 Math

Book content and design developed and published by TREND enterprises, Inc.

Printed in the United States of America

Anne M. Dunham & Debbie M. O'Neal—Writers
John R. Kober—Editor
Steven Hauge—Art Director
Lorin Walter—Designer

ISBN 1-58792-025-5

10 9 8 7 6 5 4 3 2

Ben's Birthday

Ben is excited! His birthday is coming soon. Ben has invited 4 friends to come to his birthday party. Guess where they're going?

They're going to the amusement park. Ben is glad that you are coming along too! Use the clues to name Ben's friends. Write the correct name under each person.

Clues: **Morgan** has the curliest hair in the group.
Miguel's favorite shoes are red.

Lindsay loves animals.
Katie likes to collect pins.

Ben

You

Draw yourself in the picture too.

STICKER DEED
BEN

Add the sticker of Ben to his group of friends.

2

Calendar Count

Check the calendar. Add the missing numbers.

JUNE

Sunday	Monday	Tuesday	Wednesday	Thursday	Friday	Saturday
					1	2
		5		7		9
		12				16
17		19				23
	25					30

STICKER DEED
BIRTHDAY CAKE

Ben's birthday is the 25th. Put the birthday cake sticker on that day.

How many days are in this month?_____

Number Order

Amusement Park

Ben and his friends are in line to enter the park. Number their shirts from 1 to 5.

Add the problems to finish the math maze.

$$1 + 1 = \boxed{}$$

$$\boxed{} + 2$$

$$\boxed{} + 3 = \boxed{}$$

$$\boxed{} + 4$$

$$\boxed{} + 5 = \boxed{}$$

Party Treats

Count the items to answer these questions.

1. How many lollipops?

2. How many bags of popcorn?

3. How many candy bars?

4. How many licorice ropes?

5. How many red balloons?

6. How many blue balloons?

7. How many yellow balloons?

8. How many green balloons?

STICKER DEED
COTTON CANDY

Put the cotton candy sticker in the treats stand.

All Aboard

Color the train cars to finish the pattern.

How many red cars?

How many red and blue cars?

How many red, blue, and yellow cars?

$6 + 1 = \boxed{}$

Follow the path of problems that add up to 8 to get the engine to its caboose.

START

$5 + 4 = \boxed{}$

$5 + 2 = \boxed{}$

$2 + 6 = \boxed{}$

$3 + 6 = \boxed{}$

$8 + 0 = \boxed{}$

$4 + 4 = \boxed{}$

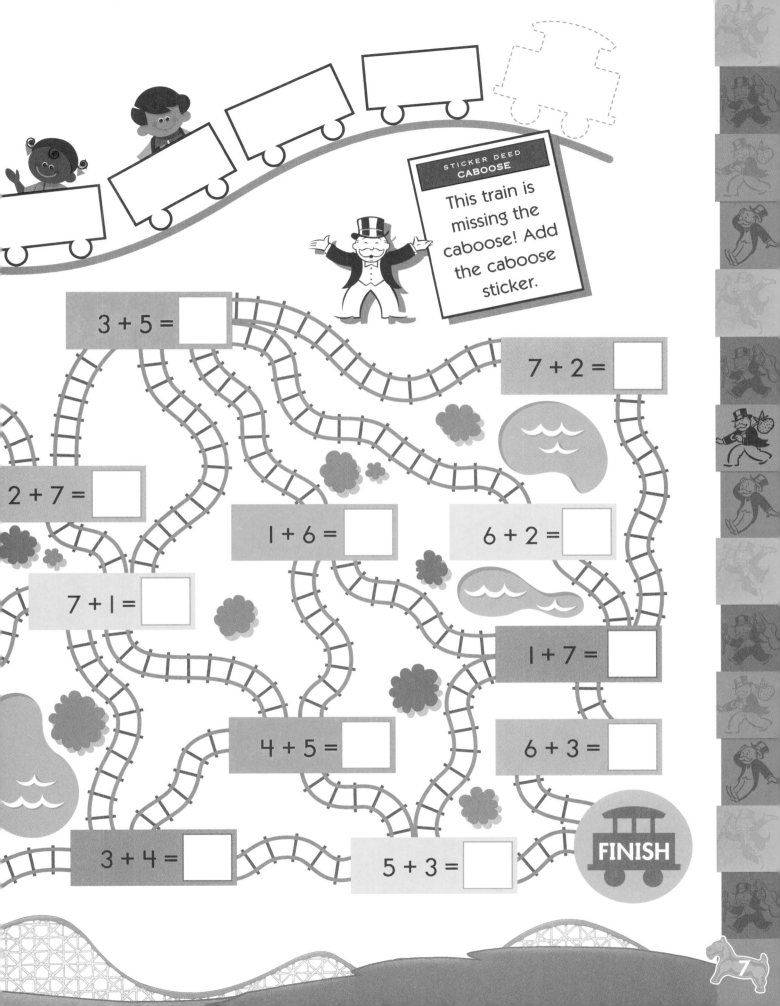

STICKER DEED
CABOOSE

This train is missing the caboose! Add the caboose sticker.

3 + 5 =

7 + 2 =

2 + 7 =

1 + 6 =

6 + 2 =

7 + 1 =

1 + 7 =

4 + 5 =

6 + 3 =

3 + 4 =

5 + 3 =

FINISH

7

Time to Go

Park Opens	10:00
Puppet Show	11:00
Magic Show	1:00
Water Show	3:00
Fireworks Show	9:00
Park Closes	10:00

Read the sign to know the park hours and the times for the shows.
Add hands to the clocks to show each of the times. Then write the time using numbers beneath each clock.

STICKER DEED
CLOCK

What time is it now? Add the clock sticker to the clock tower.

8

Magic Graphs

STICKER DEED
MAGIC HAT

The magician is missing his hat. Add the hat sticker to the magician.

Answer these questions. Use the answers to make a graph.

How many magicians? ▢

How many birds? ▢

How many rabbits? ▢

How many flowers? ▢

How many balls? ▢

Magicians					
Birds					
Rabbits					
Flowers					
Balls					

Bumper Counters

Trace the number 2 and number 6 on the cars.
Add a number to each car so they all count in order by 2s.

STICKER DEED
BUMPER CARS

Add the number 8 sticker to the correct bumper car.

| 1 | 2 | 3 | 4 | 5 | 6 | 7 | 8 | 9 | 10 | 11 | 12 |

What's for Lunch?

Hot Dog $1.00

Chips 25¢

Juice 50¢

Cookie 10¢

Ben and his friends are hungry for lunch.
How much money will they need to buy enough food for everyone?

5 hot dogs = ☐   5 juice boxes = ☐

5 bags of chips = ☐   5 cookies = ☐

Can you figure out how much it will all cost together? ☐

How much change will they get from $10.00? ☐

STICKER DEED
LUNCH MONEY

Time to pay for the food. Add the two $5.00 bill stickers to the food stand.

Lunch Subtraction

The food for lunch needs to be put on the picnic table.
Follow the directions to help put the rest of the food on the table.

X

For each of these directions, start outside the grid at the X.

1. Go over 3 squares and up 3 squares. Draw a hotdog.
2. Go over 2 squares and up 1 square. Draw a bag of chips.
3. Go over 5 squares and up 3 squares. Draw a juice box.
4. Go over 4 squares and up 1 square. Draw a hotdog.
5. Go over 1 square and up 3 squares. Draw a bag of chips.

STICKER DEED
COOKIES
Go over 3 squares and up 2 squares. Add the plate of cookies sticker.

12

Draw a picture to show each story problem. Write the answer on the line.

1. There were 15 hotdogs at the food stand. Ben bought 5 hotdogs. How many are left?

10

2. Miguel had 10 chips. He ate 3. How many are left?

3. Lindsay ate 3 cookies from the dozen. How many are left?

4. Katie finished her juice box before all the other kids. How many juice boxes are not empty yet?

5. Morgan ate all 10 of her chips. How many are left?

The kids had a great time at the picnic, until an unwelcome guest arrived for the leftovers.

STICKER DEED
LUNCH GUESTS
Guess who else came to the picnic, and add the sticker.

13

Roller Counting

Start at the ⭐ to count by 10s and connect the dots.

0	10	20	30	40	50	60	70	80	90	100
110	120	130	140	150	160	170	180	190	200	

STICKER DEED
COASTER

Add the sticker to put somone in each roller coaster car.

5, 10, 15, and More

Trace or write a number on each water plant to count by 5s up to 100.

BOAT RIDES

Haunted Math

Look carefully! Count to fill in the blanks.
Add to find the totals.

Ben saw _____ bats.

Katie saw _____ bats.

How many bats in all? _____

Morgan saw _____ candles.

Lindsay saw _____ candles.

How many candles in all? _____

Miguel saw _____ pairs of eyes in the dark.

How many eyes in all? _____

STICKER DEED
MIRROR

Find the sticker that shows what Miguel saw in the funny mirror.

Money Addition

Ben and his friends brought money to go on rides at the amusement park. How much money does each one need to go on the rides on his or her list?

Ben needs $_____.

Katie needs $_____.

Miguel needs $_____.

Lindsay needs $_____.

Morgan needs $_____.

Pony Ride— $3.00

Water Slide— $3.00

Bumper Cars— $4.00

Ferris Wheel— $4.00

Merry-Go-Round— $5.00

Ben
Pony Ride
Merry-Go-Round
Bumper Cars

Miguel
Pony Ride
Bumper Cars

Morgan
All 5 Rides

Katie
Water Slide
Ferris Wheel
Merry-Go-Round

Lindsay
Water Slide
Bumper Cars

STICKER DEED
MONEY

Find the money stickers and add them to this page.

Shopping

Look at the picture to decide how much each person will spend.

Yea!

Team!

Rah!

Go!

$2.00

$3.00

2 for $1.00

$1.00

2 for $3.00

1. Ben wants to buy a hat. How much will he spend?

2. Morgan wants to buy a stuffed bear. How much will she spend?

3. Lindsay wants to buy 4 pennants. How much will she spend?

4. Miguel wants to buy three goldfish. How much will he spend?

5. Katie wants to buy 2 toys on sticks. How much will she spend?

6. How much will the group spend all together?

STICKER DEED
FLAG

Find and add the flag sticker to the gift stand.

Toys

Money Subtraction

The kids are taking pony rides. Read the story problems and write the math sentences to solve the problems. The first one is done for you.

Pony Rides $3.00

1. Katie wants a pony ride. She has $7.00. How much money will she have left?

$7.00 – $3.00 = $4.00

2. Morgan wants a pony ride. She has $9.00. How much money will she have left?

3. Lindsay wants a pony ride. She has $11.00. How much money will she have left?

4. Miguel wants a pony ride. He has $13.00. How much money will he have left?

5. Ben wants a pony ride. He has $3.00. How much money will he have left?

STICKER DEED
PONY

Find the pony sticker and add it to the page.

Add and Subtract

Go down each water slide. Do the addition and subtraction to get an answer at the end.

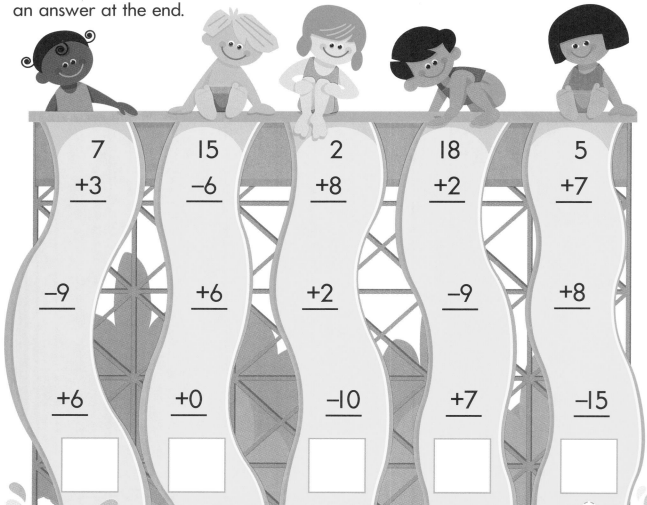

7	15	2	18	5
+3	−6	+8	+2	+7
−9	+6	+2	−9	+8
+6	+0	−10	+7	−15
☐	☐	☐	☐	☐

What do you notice about each of the final answers? _____

STICKER DEED
SPLASH!

Add the splashing kids stickers to the slides.

Count the shapes. Write how many of each shape. Use the color code to color the picture.

shapes

Red = _____

Blue = _____

Green = _____

Yellow = _____

Purple = _____

Orange = _____

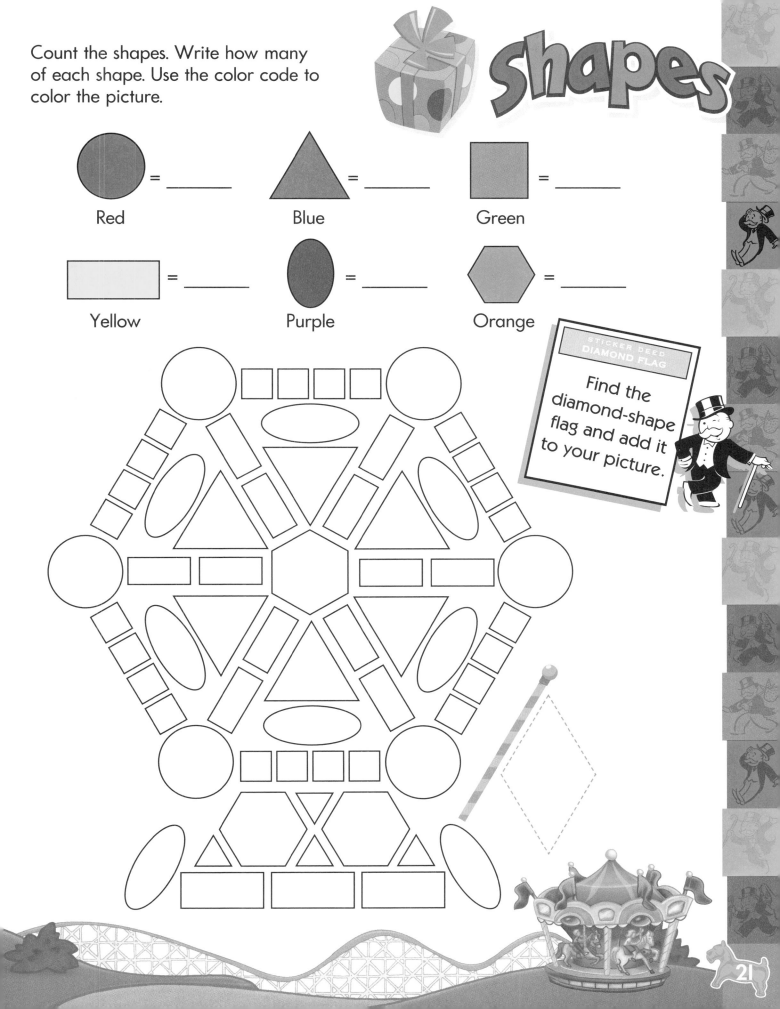

Let's Play Golf

Use the tape measure to answer the questions about how far the golf ball was hit.

1. The yellow ball was first hit 5 feet, then 3 feet, and then 2 feet. How far did the ball travel? _____

2. The green ball was hit 7 feet, then 3 feet, and 1 foot. How far did the ball travel? _____

3. The blue ball was hit 8 feet, then it rolled backwards 2 feet. Then the ball was hit another 4 feet. How many feet away did it finally end up? _____

4. The red ball made it in the hole in 3 shots. Decide how far it went on each shot, and then write a math sentence to show how far the ball traveled.

STICKER DEED
GOLF CLUB

Add the golf club sticker to finish the picture.

What Time?

Answer each question with a time that is shown on one of the clocks below.

1. It is 4:15 and Miguel has just finished playing miniature golf. He wants to go to the Ferris wheel. It will take him 15 minutes to walk there. What time will he get to the Ferris wheel?

2. Katie was anxious to get to the park today. She got up this morning 20 minutes earlier than usual. Katie usually gets up at 7:35. What time did she get up this morning?

3. The kids are meeting for lunch at noon, and then going from lunch to the magic show. What time do you think the magic show begins?

4. Morgan left the magic show at 1:45 to go to the water show that begins at 2:15. If it takes her 40 minutes to walk across the park, will she get to the water show on time?

5. The fireworks begin at 8:30 and last for 45 minutes. At what time will the fireworks end?

STICKER DEED
TELLING TIME

Find the time stickers for the clocks above and add them beneath each clock.

Count and Graph

How many 👓 sunglasses? ☐

How many 🧢 hats? ☐

How many 🐬 dolphins? ☐

How many 🦭 seals? ☐

How many 🏐 balls? ☐

How many 🎈 balloons? ☐

STICKER DEED
BALLOON HOLDERS

Who are the balloon sellers? Find and add the two stickers.

24

Color the graph to show how many of each item.

Addition Wheel

Start at the center of the Ferris wheel. Add the three numbers in each section and write the answer in the outside space.

17

6   5

8   14

10 12   3   9   15

7   5

14   7

STICKER DEED
FERRIS WHEEL

Who else is on the Ferris wheel? Find and add the sticker.

26

Adding 10s

Add the problems to find the sums. Then use the number code on the roller coaster to write letters under each sum to discover the secret message.

10 +10	20 +10	90 +10	30 +70	40 +30
20				
H				

STICKER DEED
BIRTHDAY HAT

Add the birthday hat sticker to Ben.

40 +50	20 +30	40 +40	10 +50	10 +10	30 +10	10 +20	50 +20

Number code:

90 B
100 P
80 R
70 Y
60 T
50 I
40 D
30 A
20 H

27

Subtraction Color

Solve the problems. Write the answers on the animals. Then use the answers with the color key below to finish coloring the merry-go-round.

| 12 | 17 | 12 | 14 |
| -4 | -8 | -6 | -8 |

| 16 | 15 | 10 | 11 | 18 |
| -7 | -7 | -6 | -4 | -13 |

Color Key

4 = Red   5 = Blue   6 = Green   7 = Yellow   8 = Purple   9 = Orange

28

Addition Color

Solve the addition problems.
Match the answers to the color key to add color to the fireworks.

$$\begin{array}{r} 9 \\ +5 \\ \hline \end{array}$$

$$\begin{array}{r} 5 \\ +6 \\ \hline \end{array}$$

$$\begin{array}{r} 7 \\ +6 \\ \hline \end{array}$$

$$\begin{array}{r} 8 \\ +9 \\ \hline \end{array}$$

$$\begin{array}{r} 6 \\ +6 \\ \hline \end{array}$$

$$\begin{array}{r} 9 \\ +7 \\ \hline \end{array}$$

$$\begin{array}{r} 8 \\ +7 \\ \hline \end{array}$$

$$\begin{array}{r} 7 \\ +4 \\ \hline \end{array}$$

$$\begin{array}{r} 8 \\ +3 \\ \hline \end{array}$$

$$\begin{array}{r} 4 \\ +9 \\ \hline \end{array}$$

STICKER DEED
FIREWORKS

Find the fireworks sticker and add it to the fireworks show.

Color Key

11 = Red	12 = Blue	13 = Green	14 = Purple	15 = Yellow	16 = Orange	17 = Pink

29

Birthday Treats

After the fireworks, the kids sat down for birthday cake and ice cream.
The fraction on each dish shows how much chocolate ice cream each one got.
Color the scoops to match the fraction.

STICKER DEED
CANDLE

Add the candle sticker to the birthday cake.

Birthday Fun

Ben is excited to open the birthday gifts from his friends.
Use the clues to figure out what gift each friend gave Ben.
Put a sticker on each package to identify the gift.

Ben can turn the pages of Miguel's gift.

Ben can wear Lindsay's gift.

Katie's gift has four wheels.

Morgan's gift is fun to play with friends.

Ben said,

to all his friends.

STICKER DEED
THANK YOU!

Add the
"Thank You!"
sticker to Ben's
sentence.

31

MONOPOLY

Congratulations!

This is to certify that

_____

is a
Super Math
Friend!

Mr. Monopoly™

STICKER DEED
FRIENDS

Add the sticker of Ben or one of his friends to the certificate ribbon.

Ben was so glad you shared his party at the MONOPOLY Junior Amusement Park.

Follow directions in the book to use the stickers. The extra stickers are just for fun!